Dogs Rule

Inspired by
Brittany of Shongum

Written and Illustrated by
Judy Malinchak Alberta

I am a Golden Retriever. My paws
make it difficult for me to write and I
have not yet mastered the
computer. The contents
of this book were relayed to
and entered into the computer
by my longtime friend and person,
Judy Alberta.

A special high five for the many
hours she worked
with me on this project.

Thank you, Judy,
for your inspiration,
encouragement, dedication,
friendship, and love.

Fondly,
Brit

LOVE YOUR
FAMILY
WITH
ALL YOUR
HEART
EVEN
THOUGH
THEY
MAY NOT
ALWAYS
DESERVE IT.

IT IS "EMILY POST"
CORRECT
TO
PUT YOUR
FRONT PAWS ON THE
TABLE
TO REACH SPECIAL
FOOD ITEMS.

REST YOUR
CHIN
ON THE
COFFEE TABLE
WHEN YOU
ARE TIRED.

CHEW WITH YOUR MOUTH OPEN SO UNDESIRABLE FOOD FALLS OUT EASILY.

YOU MUST BE
FIRST TO
GO UP STEPS
OR
OUT THE
DOOR.

DO
THE MAMBO
WITH A PERSON'S
LEG.

YOU OWN ALL THE SLIPPERS!

Bring fuzzy toys outside.

Bring fuzzy toys inside to dry on the rug when wet from the rain.

Frozen fuzzy toys come in to get warm and thaw.

THE STUFFING
IN
A FUZZY TOY
IS FOR
SHIPPING
PURPOSES
ONLY
AND SHOULD
BE
REMOVED UPON
ARRIVAL.

"SIT" means
roll over.
"ROLL OVER"
means lay
down.
"PAW" means
jump up.

BABIES ARE GOOD
BECAUSE THEY
DROP MOST OF
THEIR
FOOD.

BABIES ARE BAD
BECAUSE THEY
THINK THEY OWN
ALL THE TOYS.

BE NICE TO THE
BABY
BECAUSE WHEN IT
COMES TO
CHOOSING WHO
STAYS AND WHO
GOES...
THE BABY WILL
PROBABLY GET TO
STAY.

SQUIRRELS AND
CATS DON'T
RUN FAST,
SO BE SPORTING
AND
LET THEM WIN
SOME
TRACK EVENTS.

TAKE THE SQUEAK OUT OF THE SQUEAK TOY.

HANG
A DRIPPING
TONGUE
OUTSIDE
YOUR
MOUTH
TO DRY.

HIDE SHOES.

Do not take your person for a walk without his leash firmly attached to his hand. He may get lost or, worse yet, hit by a car.

WALK
SIDEWAYS.

RUIN A NEW PAIR OF STOCKINGS WITH A STROKE OF YOUR PAW.

MAKE SLURP NOISES WHEN YOU DRINK.

CHEWING YOUR FOOD BEFORE YOU SWALLOW IS RARELY DONE.

Wake your person up at 3 A.M.
Wake your person up at 4 A.M.
Wake your person up at 5 A.M.

STARING AT TABLE FOOD MAGICALLY BEAMS IT INTO YOUR MOUTH.

Hide all valuables
and forget where you hid
them.
Ancestral canines have
been doing this for years.
It is the primary reason
we have
historically important
artifacts today.

EXPECT EVERY
FAMILY MEMBER
OR
ACQUAINTANCE TO
PET YOUR HEAD
OR
SCRATCH YOUR
STOMACH
UPON ARRIVAL.

ROAD PIZZA IS SOMETIMES DINNER.

ANYTHING ON
THE
FLOOR
AUTOMATICALLY
BECOMES YOUR
PERSONAL
PROPERTY.

SPEED WALKING
AND JOGGING ARE
IN VOGUE
AND PROVEN TO BE
BENEFICIAL
FOR YOUR HEART.
INVITE YOUR
PERSON
TO JOIN YOU ON
YOUR OUTINGS.

IF HE CAN'T KEEP UP
THE PACE
HE CAN USE A
BICYCLE.

**TAIL CHASING IS
HEALTHY
AEROBIC
EXERCISE.**
BUT HEED THIS
HEALTH
WARNING:
IF YOU FEEL
FAINT OR DIZZY,
STOP
IMMEDIATELY.

REMEMBER TO CHECK WITH YOUR VET BEFORE BEGINNING ANY EXERCISE ROUTINE.

THE KING SIZE BED IS
YOUR BED.

THE QUEEN SIZE BED
IS
YOUR BED.

THE COUCH IS
YOUR BED.

IF YOU WAKE UP TIRED, YOU ARE HAVING TOO MANY RUNNING DREAMS AND MAY NEED MORE SLEEP.

LEARN TO
COMMUNICATE
USING EAR SIGNALS.
EARS UP:
I'm sort of listening to
what you are saying.
EARS DOWN:
I'm pretending to feel
sorry.
ONE EAR UP ONE EAR
DOWN:
You are not making any
sense.
EARS FORWARD:
Intruder alert.
EARS BACK:
I am very upset and
someone better rectify the
situation mighty quick.

Consider your bath to be their shower and shake vigorously near a person of your choice.

SHEDDING DOES NOT MEAN YOU ARE GOING BALD.

ALTHOUGH
DISAPPOINTING,
CHOCOLATE
BUNNIES
ARE NOT DOG
FOOD.

Chewing green grass settles your stomach.

YOU ARE THE "SOCK MONSTER" THAT IS FABLED TO LIVE IN THE WASHING MACHINE.

HALLOWEEN
IS FOR DOGS,
SO DRESS UP
AND
GO GET
TREATS
WITHOUT
DOING ANY
TRICKS.

CHRISTMAS IS FOR DOGS. EXPECT A FULL STOCKING AND LOADS OF PRESENTS.

Never assume
you are guilty.
Never look
ashamed.
Never crawl
away.
Your person is
yelling
because
someone
made a mess on
the floor.
It is his problem,
not yours.

TILTING YOUR HEAD GIVES YOUR PERSON THE IMPRESSION THAT YOU DO NOT UNDERSTAND THE COMMAND.

DO NOT CHASE CARS!

YOU COULD CATCH ONE.

Rolling in dirt
after a bath
conditions
your fur
and repairs
split ends.

YOU ARE ENTITLED TO SEVEN BIRTHDAY PARTIES A YEAR.

You are
responsible for
slowing
household
traffic
as the
Official Family
Speed Bump.

FRISBEES ARE FOR CATCHING AND CHEWING.

WIPE YOUR
FACE
AFTER MEALS
ON THE
ORIENTAL
RUG.

Remember to kick one foot wildly when someone scratches your stomach. People think it is cute and funny. Be considerate and don't disappoint them.

NO MATTER
WHAT YOU DO,
MAN WILL
ALWAYS LOVE
YOU.
THEREFORE,
YOU CAN
PRETTY MUCH
DO
WHATEVER YOU
WANT.

A dog should smell like a dog.
Not like peppermint.

Ecologically
minded dogs
dig holes;
it helps to
aerate the soil.

CAT LOVERS
ARE JUST
PEOPLE WHO
HAVEN'T
GOTTEN A
DOG YET.

YOU ARE
IMPORTANT!
REMEMBER,
YOU ARE THE
MAIN EXCUSE
FOR
INCOMPLETE
HOMEWORK
ASSIGNMENTS
AND
ODD SMELLS IN
THE HOUSE.

SHOES
TASTE
BETTER
THAN
RAWHIDE
PET CHEWS.

Don't ever let
people know
that dogs
are actually
alien beings
from Pluto
that invaded
earth
to
take advantage
of
human generosity.

TOILET WATER IS USUALLY FRESHER AND COLDER THAN WHAT'S IN YOUR WATER BOWL.

LASSIE, RIN TIN
TIN, BEETHOVEN,
MARMADUKE,
CHAMP, SHADOW,
HOOCH, and
BENJI
ARE GOOD ROLE
MODELS.

CUJO and
CERBERUS ARE
NOT GOOD ROLE
MODELS.

Make dog
angels
in the newly
fallen snow.

SPEED EATING IS AN OLYMPIC SPORT.

Hobbies are
fun!
Collect as
many burrs as
possible
when you are
camping out
or roughing it
for the night.

It is a known fact:
"A dog is man's
best friend."
A man needs a
dog.
So do women,
children, sheep,
Charlie Brown, the
blind, the lost, the
lonely, the hungry,
firemen,
policemen, and
watchmen.

DON'T GIVE A
SKUNK
ANY
ATTENTION.

ALWAYS TRY TO
PUT YOUR HEAD
OUT OF CAR
WINDOWS.

IF THE WINDOW
IS CLOSED,
CLEAN IT WITH
YOUR NOSE.

AT 60 M.P.H.
WHEN YOU ARE IN
THE CONVERTIBLE
WITH THE
TOP DOWN
AND YOUR EARS
ARE WINGED BACK
HUM YOUR
FAVORITE TUNE.

AN EFFICIENT
MASTER
SHOULD RESPOND
QUICKLY
WHEN YOU
SCRATCH THE
DOOR
TO GO OUT OR
COME IN.
BARK LOUDER
IF THE DOOR IS
NOT OPENEND
IMMEDIATELY!
HOWLING MAY BE
NECESSARY.

Wearing a
bandana is
cool.
Ribbons and
bows are cute,
ONLY
if you are
a Poodle or
Bichon Frise.

All
good watch
dogs jump
backwards and
bark loudly
at the sound of
the door bell.
Pavlov would
be so proud.

People and dogs often greet guests with an embrace and a kiss.

YOUR WATER DISH IS A SPLASH TOY.

With a little patience, you can train your person to give you unlimited treats for doing simple tricks.

WHEN THE FAMILY
GOES OUT
and
LEAVES YOU ALONE
TRY TO FIND SOME
WAY
TO LET THEM KNOW
YOU DISAPPROVE
OF THEIR ACTIONS.

LIFT YOUR
SPRITS
BY
OCCASIONALLY
SHOPPING
THROUGH THE
TRASH.
RECYCLING IS
IMPORTANT.

Baths and Vaccinations are forms of canine torture. Resist at all costs.

ALWAYS ACT LIKE
YOU ARE HAPPY
TO SEE YOUR FAMILY
WHEN THEY COME
HOME FROM SCHOOL
OR WORK EVEN
THOUGH THEY JUST
WOKE YOU UP
FROM A DEEP SLEEP.

NEWSPAPER WAS MADE FOR THREE PURPOSES:

1. SHRED
2. LAY ON
3. WET

IF YOU TAKE A
PRIVATE
AFTERNOON
STROLL,
WATCH THE TIME
AND BE HOME
BEFORE MIDNIGHT.
YOU WANT TO AVOID
THE
EMBARASSMENT OF
HAVING
YOUR PICTURE
POSTED
EVERYWHERE
WITH THE WORD
"MISSING".

BE PROUD OF YOUR
SPECIES!
CANINES BRING
COLOR TO THE
ENGLISH LANGUAGE:
A WOMAN CAN WEAR
A POODLE SKIRT
AND BE IN PUPPY
LOVE.
A PERSON CAN BE
DOG TIRED, ON A DOG
DAY AFTERNOON
AND HIS
DINNER MIGHT TASTE
LIKE DOG __ __ __ __.

POLITELY TAKE
ALL FOOD THAT IS
OFFERED TO YOU.
YOU CAN
INCONSPICUOUSLY
SPIT IT OUT
ON THE RUG
LATER WHEN NO
ONE IS LOOKING.

Gently
inform the
children
in your life that
you are
not a horse
and
they may not
ride on your
back.

THE ONLY THING WORTH BITING IS A HAMBURGER.

LISTEN
CAREFULLY TO
CONVERSATIONS.
MAKE SURE
THAT CAR TRIPS
DO NOT INCLUDE
A STOP AT THE
VETERINARIAN.

DON'T BE
A THUNDER
WIMP. YOU
CAN NOT DIG
TO CHINA VIA
THE CLOSET.

We are all
Lapsitters.
AKC registered
or not. Size
does not
matter.

WEAR EAR MUFFS ON THE 4TH OF JULY.

GLUE YOURSELF TO THE FLOOR WHEN YOU DO NOT WANT TO DO SOMETHING.

Only creatures
with two feet
are required
to wipe them
before they
enter the
house.

PLEASED:
Wag just your tail.
HAPPY:
Wag your tail and wiggle
your body.
THRILLED:
Run in large circles
EXCITED:
Pee.

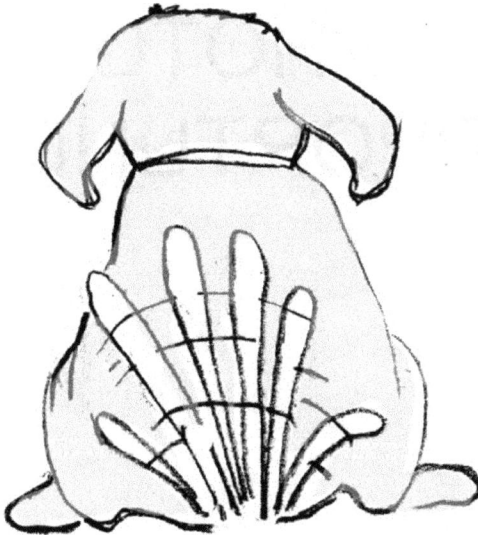

AFTERNOON
TEA WITH THE
YOUNGSTERS
AND DRESS UP
PLAY
IS A PERFECT
PHOTO
OPPORTUNITY.

REMEMER TO HIDE YOUR FACE FROM THE CAMERA SO THAT YOU WILL NOT BE RECOGNIZED ON FACEBOOK.

ANGELS OFTEN DISGUISE THEMSELVES AS DOGS.

Standing
perfectly and
walking proudly
to earn a
blue ribbon
is a small price
to pay
for being
pampered for
weeks.

YOU TOO CAN BE A FAMOUS CORPORATE ICON

Grayhound Bus
RCA
Target

When you share
your bed
with your person,
he feels safe
knowing you
are near.
So, grunt, wheeze,
snort and
push reassuringly
against his body
while you sleep.

IF ALL ELSE FAILS, GIVE SAD EYES.

REMOVE SLIDER DOOR SCREENS WITH A RHINO-LIKE CHARGE.

TELEPATHICALLY
COMMUNICATE
YOUR NEEDS
TO A PERSON
MUNCHING A
TASTY SNACK
BY GIVING THEM
"THE HOMELESS,
HUNGRY POSTER
DOG" LOOK.

ENCOURAGE YOUR
PERSON
TO EXERCISE
REGULARLY:
Ball throwing builds
arm muscles
Towel pulling relieves
back pain.
Shoe chasing
improves the
cardiovascular
system.
Step-over dog
enhances balance.

DO NOT SHOW OFF NEWLY LEARNED TRICKS ON DEMAND.

NO PERSON OR CREATURE MAY ENTER YOUR HOME WITHOUT YOUR PERMISSION.

When you hear
a can opener
motor running,
act nonchalant.

Yes, you are the watch dog but don't worry, no one will ever ask you the time.